I SPY
with my little eye...
ANIMALS!

READY? LET'S BEGIN!

LET'S CONNECT:

🌎 : PamparamKidsBooks.com

▶ : Pamparam Kids Books

Ⓟ : Pamparam Kids Books

📷 : @PamparamKidsBooks

© Copyright by Pamparam Kids Books. Images Feepik.com or licensed for commercial use. All rights reserved.

I SPY with my little eye, an animal beginning with...

i SPY with my little eye, an animal beginning with...

J

i SPY WITH MY LITTLE EYE, AN ANIMAL BEGINNING WITH...

I SPY WITH MY LITTLE EYE, AN ANIMAL BEGINNING WITH...

I SPY with my little eye, an animal beginning with...

Alligator!

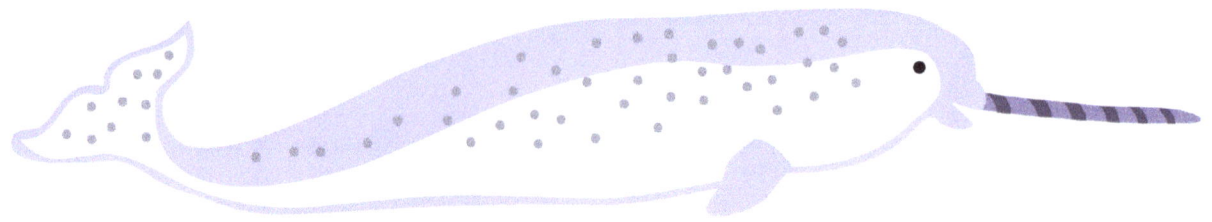

I SPY WITH MY LITTLE EYE, AN ANIMAL BEGINNING WITH...

T

i SPY WITH MY LITTLE EYE, AN ANIMAL BEGINNING WITH...

S

www.ingramcontent.com/pod-product-compliance
Lightning Source LLC
Chambersburg PA
CBHW040223040426
42333CB00051B/3429